AROUND MARSHFIELD - THEN AND NOW

by IAN S. BISHOP

INTRODUCTION

In producing this, my fourth book in the Then and Now series, I have turned to an area of high uplands which in part form The Southwolds, being the most southerly extension of the Cotswolds, and is based on and around the old and historic town of Marshfield. For reasons which are now lost in the midst of time, these uplands have been inhabited for thousands of years as many prehistoric burial grounds, in the form of long and round barrows of various types, plus Druidical Stones have been found within the vacinity of Marshfield. By the time of the Conquest, the town was recorded as Meresfelde, and was held by Queen Edith, the widow of Edward the Confessor, passing to Queen Matilda in 1075. A hundred years later it became part of the Abbey of Keynsham, where it remained for almost four hundred years. It was the Abbot of Keynsham who in 1234, obtained the right to hold weekly markets plus, a three day fair around St. Oswald's Day, despite protestations from the good citizens of Bristol. Following the dissolution of the monasteries in 1548, the manor passed through a number of hands before being divided between the Goslett's and the Crispe's.

Over the years the town grew and prospered being described by Samuel Rudder in 1789 as:

"The Town of Marshfield stands near the middle of the parish and consists chiefly of one street, near a mile long, through which a turnpike road leads from London to Bristol. The business of making malt to supply the cities of Bristol and Bath was formerly very great here, for which the town is conveniently situated in a corn country; and though it has been for some time declining yet it is still pretty considerable. The market, which is but little frequented, except in the malting season, is held on Tuesday and there are two fairs in the year, on the 24th May and 24th October, for which privileges their charter was renewed in the reign of James 1"

Malting was, for a long time, the staple trade upon which the town depended for its prosperity, a trade, which at its peak during the 15/16th centuries occupied no less than forty-three malt houses. However by the beginning of the seventeenth century, the number of maltsters had fallen to twenty-one, although the decline levelled out over the following two hundred years as sixteen maltsters were still plying their trade in 1839. The years that followed saw a fall in the prosperity of the town to the extent that during 1865 the Field Gardens were set up to provide profitable employment for the working classes and to afford hope and a fair prospect of be
were willing to help themselves
the establishment of mills in or
constructed down in the valley le
candles were made in Marshfield,
further into the valley a number of

Nowadays although the modern t ... y-pass Marshfield it retains its independence as a vibra ... ommunity, still heavily reliant upon agriculture, as well as being a dormitory area for the nearby cities. It attracts tourists and visitors alike, is well known for the "Mummers" who perform their Christmas mystery play each Boxing Day, and recently has acted as the backdrop to the BBC's period drama "Wives and Daughters".

Of the other habitations included in this book, Tormarton is the second largest and has probably been around as long as Marshfield, certainly prehistoric man has left his mark on the landscape in the form of at least one long barrow. Tormarton is a compact upland village, and as its name suggests originated as a hill top settlement on or near a boundary. At the time of the Domesday Book the Manor was held by Alric who, subsequently forfeited the estate to a Richard le Legate. By 1314 the Manor of Toremertone together with the hamlet of Luttletone was held by John de la Ryvere, whose family appears to have remained "lord of the manor" for the next four hundred years or so. After that family the manor passed through different families, until the manor was destroyed some time during the Civil War. During the time before the introduction of the combustible motor vehicle, Tormarton straddled the old coaching route between the cities of Bath and Gloucester. Although the above hamlet of Luttletone may not immediately be recognised today under that name, it will, under its modern title of West Littleton. This picturesque hamlet lies some two miles to the south of Tormarton across the M4 valley, and again is a place steeped in ancient history and the presence of habitation going back over many thousands of years.

Further south lies the pretty hamlet of Cold Ashton, whilst also included within the book are the hamlets of Hinton to the west, and North Wraxall to the east.

In preparing this book I must record my thanks to Mr. & Mrs. Leppard for their information so freely given with regard to Tormarton, and for allowing me to include their picture on page 14. Although many of the other pictures reproduced in this book have been taken from the author's own collection, I am indebted to Mike Tozer for providing additional and interesting views to be shared with you the reader. My special thanks go to my wife Doreen for accompanying me as we explored the area; for her help in matching up the Now pictures with the Then, for checking over the written word and correcting the mistakes.

July 1999 — Ian S. Bishop

This general view of Hinton is the only old commercial photograph which has so far turned-up. School children stand and stare at the photographer; cattle browse the meadow, and geese, in Indian file, cross at the rear whilst houses and cottages frame this rural scene.

The meadow has lost its somewhat manicured appearance, having been partially invaded by scrub and nettles. Although cattle still graze, the houses and the cottages have hidden themselves behind a more dense growth of trees and bushes to give an unwarranted air of neglect.

On the right can be seen the School House constructed in 1859, when the mixed Public Elementary School was built to accommodate 80 village children. At the time that the picture was taken (c1915) the master was W.J. Coombes. Beaufort Cottages are central whilst in the background is the village's general store, recently built as an extension to the *Beaufort Arms*.

Most of the buildings retain the same outward appearance, but the grass mound seen in the previous picture has gone, whilst the road has now been delineated, a pavement constructed, and openings have appeared in boundary walls to accommodate the need of modern day traffic.

Without the need to concentrate upon School House, this view of the same street shows property on both sides, with those on the left enjoying much longer front gardens and much more luxuriant vegetation. Note that the *Beaufort Arms* has yet to acquire its extension. c1905.

Pavements on both sides have been constructed and the resulting curb stones give the appearance of having straightened out the road and makes todays view much more angular than the softer curves of the previous picture. In the centre background the *Beaufort Arms* has become the *Portcullis Inn*. Street lighting has arrived and somehow the tranquillity looks more fragile.

The village has lost one of its sons, as on the 9th March 1916 Cpl. Montague Cottrell of the Gloucestershire Regiment, gassed in France, makes his final journey as he is carried by his comrades and accompanied by his family and friends. Remnants of winter's snow increase the poignancy of this last farewell.

The moving spectacle of the military funeral has long since faded with the passage of time, whilst the properties have seen countless winters come and go. Trees and bushes grow where once there was a village pond, and with cars required to complete the chores of shopping in centres miles away, the parochial heart of the community has sadly gone for ever.

One of the more dominant private houses in the village, Grange Farm acts as the backdrop to a posed picture of a gentleman in a horse-drawn trap, with two children looking on. At the time that this photograph was taken the Gent family occupied Grange Farm and, it is possible that the old gentleman proudly sitting in his trap is George Gent himself. c1904.

A large tree has now grown in the front garden and this prevents a worthwhile picture being taken from the same angle. Even so although the camera has been moved to a different position, it can still be seen that very little has changed over the past 95 years. A hedge replaces/covers the metal fencing, some ivy has been cut back, the side entrance to the property has been removed, and a pavement constructed.

A group of young men idle the day away having come to the village pump by horse, by cart, and on foot, having no doubt been attracted by the young ladies in the end house. This group of estate properties are enhanced, as is the whole village, by the three thatched cottages on the right, whilst on the left a larger house has yet to be built. c1905.

Hedges mask all but the rounded finial of the old village pump, the right-hand side of the three cottages has lost its outer companion and, having been converted into two, the whole property has been shorn of its thatched roof (unfortunately removed some time during 1963).

Rose Cottage and a proud Mum, Nellie Cottrell shows off her daughter Jean, to the camera and her neighbour Mrs. Always. Rose cottage has now been combined with the adjoining property to become one dwelling and at the same time has retained its thatched roof unlike the cottage on the extreme left. Note only two eyebrow windows in this picture compared with the three on page 12. c1938.

On a bright summers day in July 1999, Doreen shows Peter and Jean Leppard some of the old pictures of Tormarton for identification. Behind is Rose Cottage now modernized and sadly minus its thatched roof.

Across the village pond with Mr. William Russell's Post Office on the right, with an enamel advertising plaque, telling all of his agency for Brooks Dye Works. The small habitation adjoining Rose Cottage has been demolished, a public telephone is now available in the village, whilst the pump stands proudly alone like a sentinel. c1925.

The village pond was filled in some time during the early 1950's and the site now acts as a childrens play area. The old Post Office can just be glimpsed through the large trees on the right, whilst the round finial at the top of the village pump pokes above the foliage on the left.

Chestnut Farm House on the outskirts of Tormarton during the late summer of 1904, with the picture printed as a joint Christmas and New Year Card. Note hayrick on left. Careful study of the card reveals that originally the publisher intended to write the greeting on the side of the house.

With an extension built on the side, and a neatly trimmed hedge, Chestnut Farm is now a well-known local "Bed & Breakfast" venue. However attractive the property/picture is, in todays modern and sophisticated world, how many people would appreciate being the recipient of such a similarly produced festive card, although at least in 1904 the card arrived on Christmas Day.

Looking across the village pond to the edge of the local community, and the rolling north-western hills beyond, as the un-made road sweeps down the hill, and through the overflow from the pond. c1905.

Apart from the obvious fact that the pond has been completely filled-in and the road has been made-up, todays scene even after the passage of almost ninety-five years, remains virtually the same and demonstrates that, in certain places, time just seems to have stood still.

The large old mellow Manor House of Cold Ashton is believed to have been built around 1610, and was originally known as Turners Court. It formerly belonged to the Stroud family and then latterly, to the Gunning's. Possibly empty in the early years of this century, it was by 1930 occupied by Mrs. Mounsey. In its early period, the house included a consecrated chapel where Sir Bevil Granville died having been taken there wounded, following the Battle of Lansdown in 1643. Picture c1904

The substantial growth over the past ninety odd years of the large trees now denies today road users the same view of the Manor House as was afforded their predecessors. All that can now be identified is the high wall in the centre of the picture to the point where it met the opening for the farm gate, now blocked off by the construction of a new adjoining wall. Also hidden from this angle, but visible from the position of the car, is the same rear entrance.

The old church of Holy Trinity built of stone in the Perpendicular style, consisting of a chancel, clerestoried nave with three bays, a south facing porch and an embattled tower with pinnacles containing two bells. This view taken from a postcard written on the 28th May 1912.

Trees in the churchyard have grown and now spread their shade over the well manicured grass. The carnage caused by the First World War, and subsequent conflicts allowed many men from the Parish to die for their Country, and their names now share the peace of this English Churchyard on the prominent War Memorial. The left-hand path forms part of the official route of the Cotswold Way.

The central part of these Almshouses consists of a Chapel surmounted by a clock tower and spire, whilst either side are four houses. In the centre gable are carved the arms of the Crisp family who, during the early seventeenth century, paid for the construction of the building. At the left-hand gable end, there is an inscription stating that Thomas, son of Nicholas Crisp placed the stone there on 10th August 1612. Picture c1905.

Structurally, even after the passage of almost 100 years, the building and boundary walls remain the same and, no doubt the building has changed very little during the 387 years of its existence. At the gable end nearest the camera, the topmost stone records the laying of the coping stone by Nicholas son of Elias Crisp on 30th July 1619.

Twelve council employees pose for the cameraman in the midst of carrying out tar spraying at the west end of Marshfield, whilst 3 children and 2 young ladies look on. Smoke rises from the tar boiler with the chippings brought in by horse and cart. The steam tractor appears to be towing the workmen's hut. c1920.

The buildings are the same, and there is evidence of construction being carried out. The most obvious difference being the amount of motorized traffic now using the town.

The Congregational Chapel on the corner of St Martins Lane with the lens of the older camera making the row of cottages in the High Street look rather tall and narrow. A window cleaners ladder and small barrow can be seen on the right. c1910.

Trees now shield much of the chapel from view and hide the fact that in recent years this listed building has fallen from grace, is now redundant and awaits conversion to a new role in the twenty-first century. Further along, the cottages look less isolated, whilst road markings and cars modernize this picture. Note the old paving stones as seen opposite have been replaced by cheaper but much more impersonal asphalt.

On a quiet tranquil summers day around 1926 the Hebron Hall Baptist Church along side Rose Cottage basks in the afternoon sun, with the High Street busying itself as it copes with passage of three cars.

The small property in the centre of the previous picture has gone, as has the porch to Rose Cottage. Beyond the visible front garden has now been converted into the display forecourt of C.E. Davis & Co. Agricultural Engineers. Although the tall electric pole has gone a new piece of street furniture has appeared in the form of a modern bus stop.

The old Hospice is looking somewhat forlorn and worse for wear, as it stands alongside the Gospel Hall halfway along the High Street, whilst the start of Marshfields traffic problems are about to begin. c1925. NO 1932/34

The properties have been refurbished, modernized and converted into other uses, notably as town houses, with the old Gospel Hall, for example, now Chapel Cottage. Fortunately the external appearance has in the main been kept, thus retaining the basic character of the buildings. If only the continual line of parked cars could somehow be harmonized with the background.

J. Booy's grocer-shop can be clearly seen on the left as Marshfield is captured in one of its quiet spells, whilst its inhabitants try to come to terms with the calm before the storm of the Second World War descending on them. Just one person strolls in the sunshine in anticipation of what is yet to come. Note the base of each pole has been painted white as part of the air-raid black-out precautions. c1939.

The shop has now been converted into a private house, Marshfield has been at peace for over 50 years, and apart from the increase in traffic, the removal of the electric poles, and the painting of white lines, little appears to have changed during the past half century. Note the narrow turning on the left, behind the second parked car, known as Touching End Lane.

Edwin Charles Thomas, stationer and sub-Post Master, has his shop on the right, whilst the confectionery shop of E.C. Hinton, is situated a few doors away and advertises "Teas Available". As in the previous 'Then' picture, the base of the electric poles have been painted white. c1939.

The basic structure of the buildings remain the same, but subtle changes have taken place, with Marshfield Post Office having different style windows from those installed during Mr. Thomas's occupancy; Hinton's confectionery shop has now been enlarged into the Central Stores; the public may now use an outside 'phone, whilst a new attic window has appeared in the roof space of the building adjacent to the Post Office.

Looking west at the junction of the High Street and Sheepfair Lane. The large building on the left is the *White Hart* run by the landlord Michael Corbett. Outside stands an old man and four children as they jointly watch the antics of the photographer who appears to have temporarily left his bag on the right-hand pavement on another quiet day in the history of Marshfield. c1910.

From a comparatively empty street of the past, to the same street which has now become a haven for parked cars to add their own congestion to the mobility desires of the 1990's. Aloof of the vehicular changes around them, the surrounding buildings have coped with the passage of time by basically remaining the same, as they bask in the July heat of the mid-day sun.

Having turned the camera around to look eastward again, the *Angel Inn* (George King, Landlord) appears on the left, outside of which, a mother and daughter in the summer Sunday best, pose for the photographer whilst behind, a rather inquisitive dog looks on. Across the street stands the *Catherine Wheel* public house, and in the centre background the tower of St. Mary's rises above the buildings of the market square. c1905.

For todays photographer, a mother and child of the '90's walk pass the location of the old *Angel Inn*; whilst opposite stands the *Catherine Wheel* still going strong. Next to it is the Tolzey Hall, rebuilt on this site in 1693. Passing these buildings are other mothers taking their children home from school. The crocketed pinnacles on top of St. Mary's can be clearly seen in the background.

With the cameraman looking back in a westerly direction, the impressive façade of the *Catherine Wheel* now appears on the left, clearly showing its ornamental pierced stone balustrade under which is a collection of stone carved faces, and an attractive shell porch over the main entrance, all built around 300 years ago as a frontage to a much larger older building behind. c1960.

Perhaps not unexpectedly, little appears to have changed in this view over the past thirty-five years or so. Double yellow lines now restrict the parking to the right-hand side of the street, but apart from this, the more recognizable modern vehicles and the window boxes, the two views could almost be identical.

At around this point in the High Street it begins to widen out as the right-hand side of the street (looking in an easterly direction) angles back to form one side of a triangle, with Weir lane at its apex. A group of ladies/young girls queue outside the local baker's shop belonging to Isaac Wm. Hammond & Sons, with a Bristol tramways sign above the door confirming that parcels can be left, while further down "Teas with Hovis" are advertised next to the *Crown Inn*. An interesting study c1923.

By taking the camera back a few strides, the left-hand sign can be included in the picture stating that Marshfield is 103 miles from Hyde Park Corner, and that it replaces the original sign taken down during the Second World War. In those dark days it was felt that we should not give away too much helpful information to enemy paratroopers, no doubt overlooking that any paratrooper aiming for London and arriving in Marshfield would certainly have been confused, sign or no sign.

As the buildings on each side of the High Street spread apart, *The Crown* public house, (Frank Mould, landlord) built over 300 years ago can be seen on the extreme right. Hammond's bakery shields its window display from the summer sun whilst beyond other shops and pubs advertise their wares. Within this picture there are just four people occupying an otherwise deserted town. c1939

The basic configuration of the visible buildings in both pictures appear the same. *The Crown* has a new sign over its carriage entrance, hanging baskets brighten its display; Bass is no longer advertised in the bay window. Otherwise this building probably looks the same as it has for the past 200 years when, the property was enlarged with a new street frontage being added. By looking closely at the picture a small part of the roof of the original frontage can just be seen poking over the extended roof to the right of the first chimney.

Looking due West again with the original War Memorial in the centre of the picture, the photographer has posed his subjects to include a policeman; a mother and child; and a little girl in her white pinafore dress with perhaps her grandfather standing by. The new fangled automotive vehicles have arrived and can be seen in the background of this interesting view. c1923.

The town's new War Memorial now stands in place of the original; recording the names of its Sons who made the ultimate sacrifice in the defence of their Country. Facing the camera are the names of Edward Salmon; George Woodman; Albert Pullin; Charles Bodman, and others whose names shall live for ever.

Through the Market Square and around behind the Church is a hidden part of Marshfield town known as Little End, a cluster of small old cottages the nearest rank of which were lightly thatched as depicted in this photograph. c1902

Little End has joined the twentieth century but still retains its required independence and isolation from mainstream Marshfield. The cottages on the left have been modernized, and in doing so, have lost their thatched roofs. Cars occupy the narrow street whilst beyond neighbours have not lost the art of communicating with each other.

Twenty children in their Sunday Best have been asked by the photographer to stand in line across Hay Street, whilst a few adults look on at these strange antics hoping that they are hidden from the camera lens. A cart has been left outside of the *Lord Nelson* as another interesting moment in Marshfield's recent history is frozen in time. c1905

The right-hand tree in the other picture appears to be the main victim of the passage of time, taken away no doubt to allow less hindrance to todays faster traffic. White lines draw a pattern of road markings and one car occupies an otherwise empty area of Marshfield. Even so I was unable to find 20 children willing to help replicate the previous picture.

The quiet deserted Hay Street on the approach to Marshfield showing the more expensive and more recent, (in relative terms) out-of-town houses basking in the summer sunshine. c1910.

A pavement has replaced the grass verge on the left-hand side in this virtually unchanged scene, despite the passage of almost ninety years.

A panoramic view of North Wraxall with properties overlooking the valley. Note the thatched village Grain Store standing on six toadstool shaped stones in the bottom left-hand corner; long since dismantled, these stones can still be seen in the grounds of *The Shoe* public house. Taken from a card postally used in July 1936.

The growth of the foliage has made it impossible to replicate the earlier picture, and we are left with glimpses of just one or two recognizable parts of the buildings through the branches.

Below: said to be at Hinton, can any reader please confirm.
Right: Marshfield High Street believed to be during the winter of 1947.

JUST A GLIMPSE

Above and Right: At Tormarton around 1925.